FOREWORD

The Barberpole Cat Program

In 1971, International President Ralph Ribble launched a Society activity known as the Barberpole Cat Program. Its purpose is to encourage as many Barbershoppers as possible to become involved in quartet singing. The goal is not necessarily the formation of registered quartets, although that would be a great result if it were to happen. Rather, the program introduces men to the joy of singing with three other guys.

Since then, the Barberpole Cat Program has been consistently successful. The current list of 12 songs was selected in 1987 by a vote of Society members.

We hope the Barberpole Cat will become your favorite animal!

Music Publications Department
Barbershop Harmony Society

Table of Contents

My Wild Irish Rose	3
Wait Till The Sun Shines, Nellie	4
Sweet And Lovely (That's What You Are To Me)	6
Down Our Way	8
Honey - Little 'Lize Medley	9
Let Me Call You Sweetheart	10
Sweet, Sweet Roses Of Morn	11
Shine On Me	13
The Story Of The Rose (Heart Of My Heart)	14
You're The Flower Of My Heart, Sweet Adeline	15
Down By The Old Mill Stream	16
You Tell Me Your Dream	17
(Tags) Give Me Your Hand/Ring, Ring The Banjo	18

Purposes of the Program

- To encourage quartet activity at chapter meetings.

- To provide Barbershoppers with a common repertoire of songs that they can sing together with any three other Society members at inter-chapter activities, conventions, and other barbershopping events.

- To enable Barbershoppers to gain confidence in performing in a quartet in an informal, supportive atmosphere.

- To teach Barbershoppers a repertoire of easy arrangements that a beginning quartet can perform.

© Copyright 1992, 2015

Published by the Barbershop Harmony Society

How the program works

There are many ways in which the Barberpole Cat program can be used by the chapter to encourage quartet singing. Here is one way:

The Music Leadership Team presents to the chapter board a proposal to begin the Barberpole Cat Program. A successful Barberpole Cat Program requires the cooperation of the program vice president, the music director, and other members of the Music Leadership Team. Therefore, board approval is needed so that the required modest expenditure of funds can be appropriated and a regular time period allotted for the program during chapter meetings.

Each chapter member who participates in the program should have a copy of this book Stock no. 209064 (formerly #6053)(print) or Stock no. 209925 (digital Ebook), available through The Society. Included with the book are all individual program materials except awards.

The music director or an assistant presents the songs so that members can learn their parts in a group. The songs may be presented one at a time or in groups of two or three. Spend about five minutes per song and review each song for about five minutes during the succeeding three weeks.

The quartet teaching method can be used to advantage with the Barberpole Cat Program. If talent is available, more than one teaching quartet may be used. Review should be continued, as needed, as songs are learned. As the teaching quartet accurately sings each song without music, the quartet members automatically qualify for each song sung. Members of this group will probably be the first in the chapter to earn their Barberpole Cat pins.

A suggestion: Since there are twelve songs, it might be logical to present one song each month. By the end of a year, all of the Barberpole Cat songs could be learned.

Each week, there should be an opportunity for members to qualify on the songs. Since singing in quartets can speed the learning process, members may wish to practice their parts with three other men with music in hand in front of the chapter. Listening to the parts being sung by the quartet will help others gain familiarity with the music.

When a member teels that he can sing his part to one of the songs without the music, he may volunteer to do so in a quartet in front of the chapter. A section leader, another member of the music leadership team, or a barbershopper who is experienced in that voice part should listen to the volunteer's performance to determine whether he has sung the words and music correctly.

Songs may be learned and sung by chapter members in any order. Members may learn more than one voice part. There is no set pattern.

The entire program should be carried out in a spirit of support, fellowship, and fun. If determination is made that the volunteer has not sung the song satisfactorily, he should be praised for making the attempt and encouraged to take another look at the music or listen to a learning tape, and try the song again at the next meeting. It should be pointed out to the membership that failing is an important part of the leaming process. Each member should be encouraged to try to sing his part in a quartet.

Set reasonable standards for successful performance, then do not bend those rules. Qualifying should not be automatic.

Forms for recording individual qualifications and ordering of group awards are included in the back of this book. The quartet activity chairman should keep careful records and may wish to make copies of these documents for that purpose. See page 2, Awards.

After a year or so, interest may wane, as most members of the chapter learn all twelve songs. The program can still be continued, perhaps on a monthly basis or at whatever frequency is desired, as new members join the chapter and want to participate.

Awards

When a member successfully sings his voice part to one of the Barberpole Cat songs, he should, in addition to having his individual record sheet updated, be applauded and have his name placed on a chart, with credit for that song indicated. The chart should be displayed prominently, so that all chapter members can observe everyone's progress toward the goal of learning all twelve songs. A special chart for this purpose may be ordered from The Society's website (www.barbershop.org/polecats). Alternatively, the chapter may want to create its own chart.

Upon completion of the first six songs, the member can receive a Barberpole Cat certificate. When the member completes all twelve songs, he is eligible to receive a Barberpole Cat lapel pin. Both are free of charge. To obtain the certificates and pins, the chapter quartet activity chairman fills out a **Barberpole Cat Program Report Form** included in the back of this book, and has the chapter secretary send the form to the international office.

Award certificates and pins should be presented with appropriate fanfare.

Members who become certified Barberpole Cats will enjoy singing the songs with other chapter members and with Barbershoppers they meet at Society activities. Once they experience the joy of singing in a quartet, they may want to become involved in other quartet activities.

Other way to use the program

The Barberpole Cat program can be adapted to suit individual chapter needs and preferences.

The learning/qualifying program can be set aside and the songs used to promote informal singing. Instead of being presented as part of the chapter meeting, the program can be a separate break-out session. Or, it can be an "early-bird" program, presented before the chapter meeting. It should be pointed out, however, that there is value in the enthusiastic support of other chapter members when the program is part of the chapter meeting.

Awards can be eliminated, or additional awards may be devised by the chapter. For example, a tshirt could be awarded to members who learn all four voice parts to the twelve songs.

While a point will be reached at which there is no longer interest in presenting the Barberpole Cat program each week, the chapter may still wish to continue quartet promotion. One method of doing this is by creation of a similar program, using chorus repertoire songs instead of the Barberpole Cat series. A similar set of awards, using pins, cloth sew-on patches, tshirts, or other incentives can be devised. A chapter logo or some other design may be substituted for the Barberpole Cat emblem on these prizes.

Learning Tracks

Learning Tracks that include the twelve Barberpole Cat songs are available through The Society. Each part's learning track plays that part predominantly in the left channel while the other three voice parts will play at a lower volume level in the right channel. You will be able to adjust the left/right balance in order to hear more or less of your part-predominant channel and sing along with just your own track, or sing along with the other three parts as though you were in a quartet.

Visit www.barbershop.org/polecats to order these learning tracks and learn more about the program.

WAIT TILL THE SUN SHINES, NELLIE
1905

Words by ANDREW B. STERLING (1874-1955) Music by HARRY VON TILZER (1872-1946)
Arranged by Warren "Buzz" Haeger

Copyright © 1986 SPEBSQSA, Inc. (Barbershop Harmony Society)
110 Seventh Avenue North, Nashville, TN 37023-3704
All Rights Reserved.

SWEET AND LOVELY
(THAT'S WHAT YOU ARE TO ME)
1971

Words and Music by
NORMAN STARKS
Arranged by Mac Huff

Copyright © 1971 SPEBSQSA, Inc. (Barbershop Harmony Society)
110 Seventh Avenue North, Nashville, TN 37023-3704
All Rights Reserved.

DOWN OUR WAY
1927

Words and Music by
AL STEDMAN and FRED HUGHES
Arranged by Floyd Connett

Copyright © 1959 SPEBSQSA, Inc. (Barbershop Harmony Society)
110 Seventh Avenue North, Nashville, TN 37023-3704
All Rights Reserved.

LET ME CALL YOU SWEETHEART

Words by BETH SLATER WHITSON

Music by LEO FRIEDMAN

SWEET, SWEET ROSES OF MORN

Words and Music by
OSCAR F. JONES
and MARTIN S. PEAKE
Arranged by Floyd Connett

Copyright © 1959 SPEBSQSA, Inc. (Barbershop Harmony Society)
110 Seventh Avenue North, Nashville, TN 37023-3704
All Rights Reserved.

SHINE ON ME

TRADITIONAL SPIRITUAL
Arranged by Floyd Connett

Copyright © 1959 SPEBSQSA, Inc. (Barbershop Harmony Society)
110 Seventh Avenue North, Nashville, TN 37023-3704
All Rights Reserved.

THE STORY OF THE ROSE
(HEART OF MY HEART)
1899

Words by "ALICE"
Music by ANDREW MACK (1863-1931)
Arranged by Barbershop Harmony Society

Copyright © 1973 SPEBSQSA, Inc. (Barbershop Harmony Society)
110 Seventh Avenue North, Nashville, TN 37023-3704
All Rights Reserved.

YOU'RE THE FLOWER OF MY HEART, SWEET ADELINE
1903

Words by RICHARD H. GERARD (1876-1948)

Music by HARRY ARMSTRONG (1879-1951)
Arranged by Barbershop Harmony Society

Copyright © 1973 SPEBSQSA, Inc. (Barbershop Harmony Society)
110 Seventh Avenue North, Nashville, TN 37023-3704
All Rights Reserved.

DOWN BY THE OLD MILL STREAM

Words and Music by
TELL TAYLOR

Copyright © 1986 SPEBSQSA, Inc. (Barbershop Harmony Society)
110 Seventh Avenue North, Nashville, TN 37023-3704
All Rights Reserved.

YOU TELL ME YOUR DREAM
1899

Words by SEYMOUR A. RICE
and ALBERT H. BROWN

Music by CHARLES N. DANIELS (1878-1943)
Arranged by Phil Embury

Chorus

You had a dream, well, I had one, too;

I know mine's best 'cause it was of you.

Come, sweet-heart, tell me, now is the time;

You tell me your dream, I'll tell you mine.

Tag

You tell me your dream, I'll tell you mine.

Copyright © 1959 SPEBSQSA, Inc. (Barbershop Harmony Society)
110 Seventh Avenue North, Nashville, TN 37023-3704
All Rights Reserved.

GIVE ME YOUR HAND

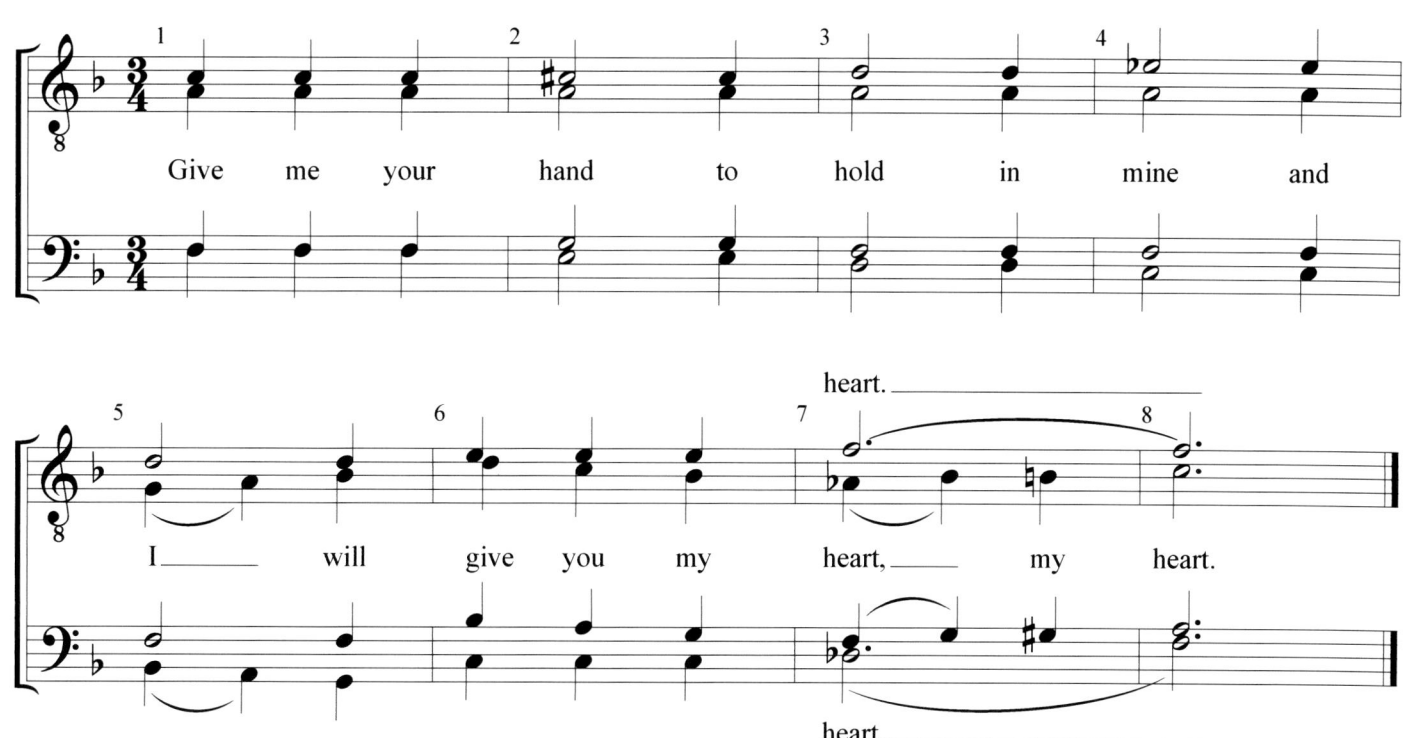

RING, RING THE BANJO

Barberpole Cat Program
INDIVIDUAL RECORD

Name _____

Chapter _____

Song   **Date qualified**

1. My Wild Irish Rose .... _____

2. Wait 'Til The Sun Shines, Nellie .... _____

3. Sweet And Lovely (That's What You Are To Me) ..... _____

4. Down Our Way .... _____

5. Honey - Little 'Lize Medley .... _____

6. Let Me Call You Sweetheart .... _____

Send for Barberpole Cat Certificate _____ **Date sent for**

_____ **Date presented**

7. Sweet, Sweet Roses Of Morn .... _____

8. Shine On Me .... _____

9. The Story Of The Rose (Heart Of My Heart) .... _____

10. You're The Flower Of My Heart, Sweet Adeline .... _____

11. Down By The Old Mill Stream .... _____

12. You Tell Me Your Dream .... _____

Send for Barberpole Cat Tie Tac _____ **Date sent for**

_____ **Date presented**

Quartet Activity Chairman _____

Barberpole Cat Program
REPORT FORM

Barbershop Harmony Society
110 7th Ave. North
Nashville, TN 37203

Please send Barberpole Cat Certificates and Tie Tacs for the following Barbershoppers in our chapter who have qualified as indicated (check appropriate column for each man).

Name _____ Certificate _____ Tie Tac _____

Name _____ Certificate _____ Tie Tac _____

Name _____ Certificate _____ Tie Tac _____

Name _____ Certificate _____ Tie Tac _____

Name _____ Certificate _____ Tie Tac _____

Name _____ Certificate _____ Tie Tac _____

Name _____ Certificate _____ Tie Tac _____

Name _____ Certificate _____ Tie Tac _____

Name _____ Certificate _____ Tie Tac _____

Name _____ Certificate _____ Tie Tac _____

Name _____ Certificate _____ Tie Tac _____

Name _____ Certificate _____ Tie Tac _____

Name _____ Certificate _____ Tie Tac _____

Name _____ Certificate _____ Tie Tac _____

Name _____ Certificate _____ Tie Tac _____

Chapter Quartet Activity Chairman _____

Chapter _____ District _____

Date _____